TRIALS AND TRIUMPHS:
The Story of
African-Canadians

LAWRENCE HILL

UMBRELLA PRESS
56 Rivercourt Boulevard
Toronto, ON
M4J 3A4

This book is dedicated to my father, Daniel G. Hill III, who taught me the pleasures of history and story telling.

TRIALS AND TRIUMPHS:
The Story of African-Canadians

Copyright © 1993 by Lawrence Hill. All rights reserved.

PUBLISHER: Kenneth H. Pearson

EDITOR: Jocelyn Smyth

DESIGN AND LAYOUT: Catherine Gordon

LINOTYPE: Robin Brass Studio

ARTWORK OF NORTH STAR: Dan Kangas

COVER: Contemporary photograph of students – Bill Ivy
Historical photograph – The children of School Section #13,
North Buxton, Ontario, photographed about 1910.
Metropolitan Toronto Library Board

Hill, Lawrence, 1957–
Trials and triumphs : the story of African-Canadians
(Peoples of Canada) Includes bibliographical references and index.
ISBN 1-895642-01-9
1. Black Canadians.* I. Title. II. Series.
FC106.B6H5 1993   971'.004036   C92-093370-X
F1035.N3H5 1993

Printed and bound in Canada

PUBLISHER:
UMBRELLA PRESS
56 Rivercourt Blvd.
Toronto, ON.
M4J 3A4
Telephone: (416) 696 6665
Fax: (416) 696 9189

Acknowledgements

In researching and writing this book, I came across many people who knew a great deal about the history about African-Canadians. They never hesitated to share their ideas and insights, and they never asked for anything in return. However, I suspect that all of them were hoping for one important service: they wanted to see the publication of a good book for young people about the trials and triumphs of Black people in Canada. I hope that they, and their children and grandchildren, will be pleased with the result.

I wish to thank the following people for their generous assistance:

Leo Bertley, Henry Bishop, Leonard Braithwaite, Vicky Brooks-Johnson, Fran and Wilson Brooks, Phyllis Brooks, Daniel Caudeiron, Lois Cox, Rita Cox, John Craig, Dr. Pat Daenzer, Dr. Daniel Hill, Donna Hill, Karen Hill, Dan Hill, Lorraine Hubbard, Jude Kelly, Daurene Lewis, Paul McLaughlin, Charis Newton, Dr. Gabriele Scardellato, Adrienne Shadd, Elizabeth Thompson, Robert Upshaw, Dr. James Walker and Dr. Ouida Wright.

Lawrence Hill

Preface

Black Canadians are also known as African-Canadians. Whether they were born in Canada, in the Caribbean or in other parts of the world, they have African ancestors, and the name African-Canadian is a proud way to remember their history. Many people like to be known as African-Canadians; others prefer to be called Blacks. In this book, both terms will be used.

Contents

CANADA

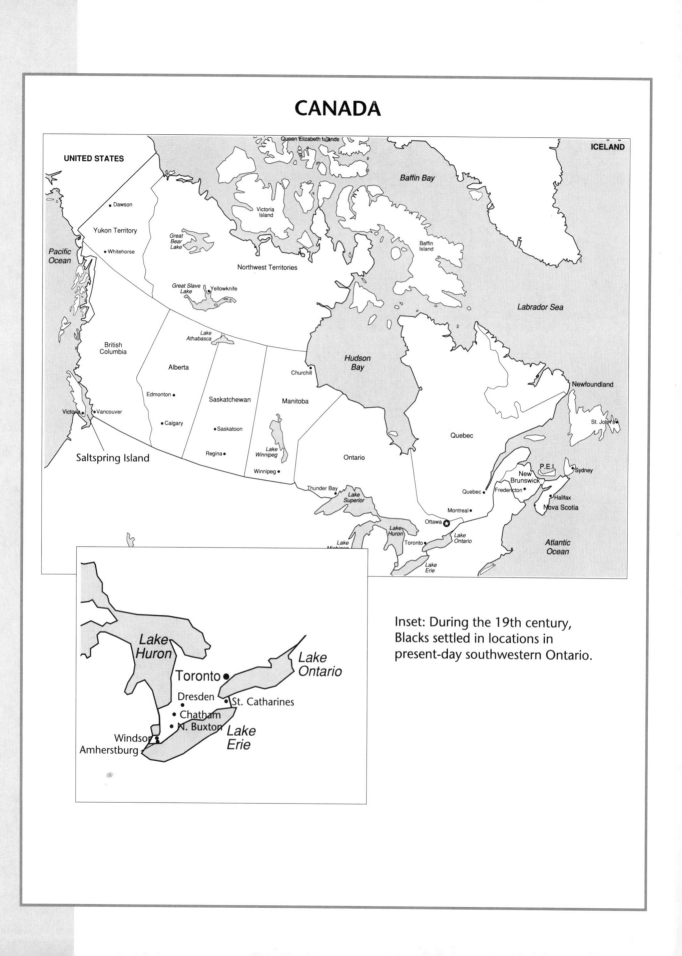

Inset: During the 19th century, Blacks settled in locations in present-day southwestern Ontario.

CHAPTER ONE

Canada: A Bit of Every Country

Black people have lived in Canada for 400 years. Like other Canadians, they have come here from many countries and in many ways. Some were brought on boats long ago. Others drove horse-drawn wagons, or walked into Canada from the United States. A few Black Americans wanted to come so badly that they arrived by swimming across the Detroit River.

Some Black people came to Canada as slaves, but most have been free men and women who came in search of dreams. Like other immigrants who settled in Canada over the centuries, Black people came to start their lives all over again. They were looking for work, new homes, new friends and new schools. They were looking for a country where all men and women could live in freedom and be treated as equals.

Black Canadians have had trials and triumphs in this country. In the early days, some lived their whole lives as slaves. Both before and after slavery was abolished, those who were free faced other hardships. Some were settled as farmers on rocky land where nothing much would grow. Others who had been promised land received none at all. Throughout their history in Canada, many have had to contend with prejudice and discrimination. For a long time, some public schools in Nova Scotia and Ontario refused to accept their children; many employers refused to hire them; property owners often refused to sell or rent them homes; and government policies made it difficult for them to bring their families to Canada. But Black Canadians overcame these obstacles one by one.

They survived, doing whatever kind of work they could get. They won a long struggle for the right to send their children to any school in the country. It became much easier for them to find homes. They have done well at all kinds of work — as carpenters, teachers, nurses, doctors, politicians, artists, engineers. They have joined hands with other people in helping to make Canada a good place to live, and that is a great triumph.

Today, Black Canadians live in every part of the country, from Newfoundland to Yukon. Some come from families that have been here for centuries, while others just arrived last year. But they all want to build good lives for themselves and their children, which is a value they share with other Canadians.

CHAPTER TWO

Africa: A Cradle of Civilization

Blacks live across Canada and around the world, but wherever they live, they have ancestors who came from Africa. Africa has been called a cradle of civilization because some of the most ancient human civilizations developed there.

Thousands of years ago, people began planting crops in the Nile River valley. Later, they started building houses with mud walls, wooden doors, and windows. Bit by bit, swampy jungle was transformed into fertile farmland all along the river valley, and a stable society with millions of people developed. Known as Egypt, this society became the most famous African civilization, and many of its citizens were Blacks. Egyptians were responsible for many important inventions and discoveries. They made use of astronomy to predict when tides would rise and fall. They devised our modern calendar system with 365$\frac{1}{4}$ days to the year, broken down into 12 months. As well, they built the pyramids—one of the wonders of the world.

Egypt was just one of the many civilizations that Africans created. Another was the Kingdom of Mali. Built in West Africa by the Mandinka people, it lasted from the thirteenth to the fifteenth century and became one of the biggest empires in the world. Mansa Kankan Musa was a rich and famous king of Mali. He had 10,000 horses in his stables. In 1324, Musa made a religious trip to Mecca, the sacred Muslim city in present-day Saudi Arabia. He brought along thousands of people and such great amounts of gold that he amazed the Egyptians with his wealth when he stopped in Cairo on his way. It is said that the king gave gold to everybody he met there, leaving so much behind that he made its price fall.

African kingdoms and cities sometimes became powerful by controlling trade routes. Traders travelled long distances to buy and sell salt, gold and other goods, and great riches could be made by controlling such traffic. Some trade routes crossed the interior of Africa and some

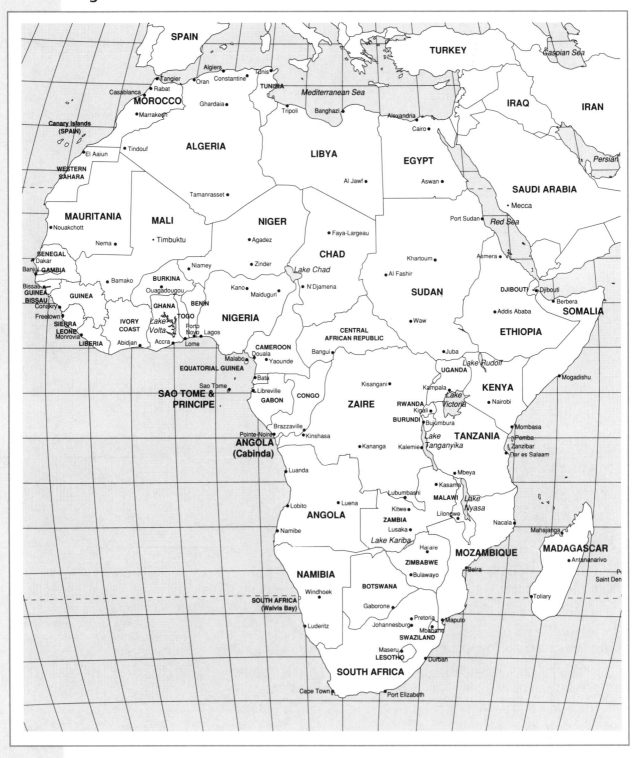

connected African coastal cities to other continents. The Swahili people on the east coast of Africa, for example, prospered by trading gold, ivory, fish and agricultural products for goods shipped from as far away as China.

Since the fifteenth century, when Europeans started travelling often to Africa, the continent has changed a great deal. Europeans controlled Africa for hundreds of years, and generally speaking, many Africans suffered greatly. It was only in the last half of the twentieth century that most African nations won back their political independence.

Like people on other continents, millions of Africans work hard, have good food to eat and live in good homes full of talking and laughter. Many old traditions, languages and cultures have survived in Africa, making it a continent with a great sense of history. The ways Africans design buildings, the ways they make music, their long history of storytelling, and their skills in countless other areas show that they have given a lot to human civilization.

Africa is the world's second biggest continent. About three times the size of Canada, it has more than 50 countries today, and about 700 million people. Sudan is Africa's largest country; Nigeria is the most populated, with about 120 million people. Some Africans live in huge cities such as Cairo, Lagos, and Kinshasa, others work as farmers in remote villages. They have many cultures, religions and ways of life. Most Africans are Black, but people of Arab, Asian and European origin also live on the continent. Africans speak more than a thousand languages. Among the most widely spoken are Swahili in the east, Hausa in the west and Arabic in the north.

CHAPTER THREE

Slavery in Canada

Slavery is almost as old as human civilization. Slaves are people whose freedom has been stolen against their will. They are forced to do other people's work without pay, and they have no freedom. A slave is another person's property, or chattel, sometimes treated worse than a work animal. That makes slavery one of the most horrible creations in the history of the world.

Rulers in ancient empires were using slaves thousands of years ago. When wars were fought, the winners often took the losers as slaves—and that included men, women, and children. Slavery has existed in every type of society and in virtually every part of the world, including Europe, Asia and Africa. Even in the days before Europeans came to Canada, some Native people had slaves or were held as slaves themselves.

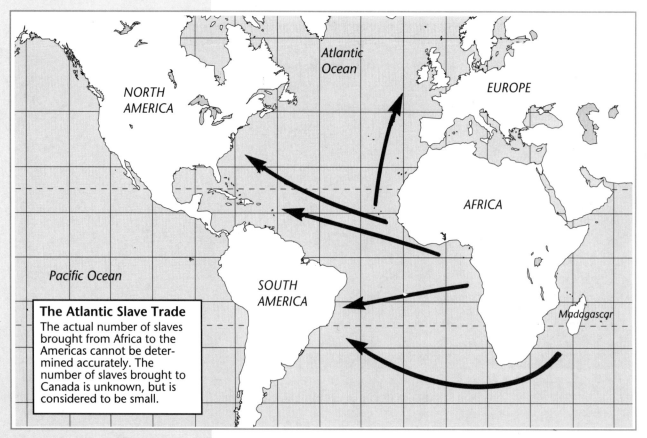

The Atlantic Slave Trade
The actual number of slaves brought from Africa to the Americas cannot be determined accurately. The number of slaves brought to Canada is unknown, but is considered to be small.

The Atlantic Slave Trade

The most vicious form of slavery that the world has ever seen was called the Atlantic slave trade. It began in the early 1600s, when Portuguese merchants sent the first shipload of Black Africans across the Atlantic to work as slaves on plantations in the New World. Soon other European traders were also taking slaves across the ocean to meet the need for masses of workers. By the time the Atlantic slave trade ended about 350 years later, millions of Africans had been captured in their villages, chained into boats and transported like animals to the Caribbean islands and to North and South America. Countless

Ankle irons and the ball and chain were inhumanely used on slaves.

others died at sea. Of those who survived the trip, many were chained, whipped or even maimed to break their spirit and to make them obey their masters. Most were forced to do back-breaking work. Children were often sold away from their parents; husbands from their wives. Once a family was torn apart, its members rarely had a chance to meet again.

Most African slaves were taken in the coastal inland areas of West Africa, from Senegal in the north to Angola several thousand kilometres to the south. Some, however,

Slaves were transported in the most inhuman, overcrowded conditions imaginable. Because of the conditions, many slaves died on board ship.

were captured far inside the continent, and a small number came from East African areas, such as Madagascar and Mozambique.

Slavery in New France

Throughout Canada's history as a French colony, slavery was accepted as a normal part of life. There were never a great many slaves in New France—or, later, anywhere else in Canada—certainly nowhere near the number there were in the United States or in the Caribbean. One reason was the long Canadian winter, which made it uneconomical to use slaves as farm labour.

The first known Black resident of Canada was an eight-year-old boy from the island of Madagascar off the East African coast. The boy was the slave of David Kirke, the English privateer who attacked Quebec in 1628. Kirke sold the boy to a local colonist who had him baptized and given the name Olivier Le Jeune.

In all, it is estimated that by the time the British conquered New France in 1759, between 1,000 and 1,500 Black slaves had come into the colony. Only a few were brought directly from Africa. Most came from the British colonies to the south or from the Caribbean islands. The majority lived in or near Montreal and Quebec City, and worked as *domestiques*, or house servants. Some, however, were bought to do the heavy work at a French fur-trading post on the Detroit River, and others worked at the French fortress of Louisbourg on Cape Breton Island.

Among the slave-owners of New France can be counted many merchants and traders, several governors (including the Marquis de Vaudreuil, the colony's last governor general), at least three bishops and even a few parish priests. As well, women's religious orders used Black slave labour at the hospitals and schools they operated.

Some slaves died while rebelling against slavery. In 1734, a Montreal woman named Marie-Joseph Angelique set fire to her owner's house to cover her escape when she learned she was about to be sold elsewhere. The fire spread, destroying 46 homes. When Angelique was caught, her hand was cut off and she was hanged.

It is also to be noted that most Black slaves died young—their average age at death was 25.

Olivier Le Jeune was the first African-Canadian. He came to Quebec in 1628 as an eight-year-old slave from Madagascar, and he lived the rest of his life in Canada. After arriving, Le Jeune was converted to the Catholic faith and baptized. When he died in 1654, he was known as a *domestique*, which is the French word for "servant". That means that he had probably been freed from slavery.

Slavery in English Canada

Nothing changed for New France's Black slaves when the colony officially passed into British hands in 1763. They remained their owners' property, and in fact, General Murray, the first British governor was a slave-owner—as would be several government officials for the next few decades.

By 1763, mainland Nova Scotia had been in British hands for 50 years. Settlers from New England had moved in after the British took the area over from France, and they may well have brought some Black slaves with them. It is known that Black slaves were among the skilled workers who built Halifax. In 1767, more than a hundred slaves lived in Nova Scotia.

The number of Black slaves in Canada suddenly rose after the Americans won their War of Independence against Britain in 1783. Not all Americans had favoured independence, and many of those who wanted to remain British subjects left the new United States of America and moved to Canada. These people were known as United Empire Loyalists, and they brought about 2,000 slaves with them. The majority settled in Nova Scotia, but significant numbers went to Quebec. The governor there sent most of them off to open up new land in what would become Upper Canada and, eventually, Ontario.

This advertisement appeared in *The Royal Gazette And The Nova Scotia Advertiser.*

Prominent Loyalist slave-owners included Sir John Wentworth, Lieutenant-Governor of Nova Scotia from 1792 to 1808, and Peter Russell, who became the Administrator of Upper Canada in 1796. Even Joseph Brant, a famous Mohawk chief whose loyalty to Britain during the American War of Independence was rewarded with a large grant of land in southwestern Ontario, owned about 30 slaves. But he also let free Blacks live on his land and marry his people.

The End of Slavery in Canada

During the second half of the eighteenth century, a growing number of people in the British Empire and elsewhere were beginning to speak out against slavery. Among the voices raised against the practice in the British Parliament was that of John Graves Simcoe, who became Lieutenant-Governor of Upper Canada in 1791. During his few years in Canada, Simcoe tried hard to get a law passed outlawing slavery. He didn't succeed entirely, because of opposition from slave-owning members of the legislature. But in 1793 he did get a law passed that forbade the import of slaves into Upper Canada and provided that any child born to a slave in Upper Canada would become free at age 25. While it did not free anyone who was already a slave, the law did ensure a gradual end to slavery in Upper Canada.

While no such law was passed in the other Canadian provinces, slavery began to dwindle away there too, helped along by the actions of a few influential people. In Lower Canada, as Quebec was called at the time, Chief Justice

JOHN GRAVES SIMCOE

Simcoe was born in 1752 in England and his career was spent as an army officer, colonial administrator, and, for a short period, as an elected politician. He served with the British forces during the American Revolution, and following the War he was elected to the British House of Commons. There he took a voice in the cause of the abolition of the slave trade.

In 1792, Simcoe arrived in Upper Canada in his position as Lieutenant-Governor. Among his accomplishments was the passage of legislation limiting slavery in Upper Canada. Although he was forced to settle for a gradual, rather than an immediate abolition of slavery, he made a significant contribution to the abolition movement.

TO BE SOLD,

A BLACK WOMAN, named
PEGGY, aged about forty years ; and a
Black boy her fon, named JUPITER, aged
about fifteen years, both of them the property of the
Subfcriber.

The Woman is a tolerable Cook and wafher woman
and perfectly underftands making Soap and Candles.

The Boy is tall and ftrong of his age, and has been
employed in Country bufinefs, but brought up prin-
cipally as a Houfe Servant—They are each of them
Servants for life. The Price for the Wowan is one
hundred and fifty Dollars—for the Boy two hundred
Dollars, payable in three years with Intereft from the
day of Sale and to be properly fecured by Bond &c.—
But one fourth lefs will be taken in ready Money.

PETER RUSSELL.

York, Feb. 10th 1806.

In 1808, Peter Russell, who had been the administrator of the government of Upper Canada, placed this advertisement in the Upper Canada Gazette.

William Osgoode helped hasten its end by refusing to convict runaway slaves. Ward Chipman, a White lawyer, politician and judge from New Brunswick, argued strongly against slavery in a court case in 1800. Chipman didn't win the case, but his arguments helped make slavery disappear in the province.

By the time Britain abolished slavery throughout the Empire in 1834, there were only a few elderly slaves remaining in Canada.

CHAPTER FOUR

African-Canadian Settlers and Immigrants

Long before slavery ended in Canada, many African-Canadians were free. Some were born free, and others were set free by their owners. Many were escaped slaves from the United States who became free when they arrived in Canada.

Two people of African origin were involved in the establishment of Port Royal, in present-day Nova Scotia. One of them soon died of scurvy, and his name is not known. The other was Mattieu da Costa, who arrived in 1606 when the little colony was in its second year. It seems likely that da Costa had made earlier trips to the area since part of his work was to serve as interpreter between Samuel de Champlain and the local Micmac people. Da Costa was a member of The Order of Good Cheer, Canada's first social club. In order to keep up morale during the long hard winters, members took turns providing an evening of good food and entertainment for the rest of the group.

Black Loyalists

The first large-scale influx of free Black people into Canada occurred at the end of the American Revolution.

During the war, Britain promised freedom to any Black slaves who joined its forces. Not surprisingly, many jumped at the chance, and when Loyalists fled to Canada after the American victory, their numbers included about 3,500 free Blacks. A few went to Upper Canada, but the majority settled in Nova Scotia. Most were bitterly disappointed in what they found there.

Like other Loyalists, Blacks had been promised farmland and supplies to get them started. Some got rocky, infertile land in isolated locations; others got none at all. Very little was done to help them get established and many suffered great hardships.

Nova Scotia's Black Loyalists were not the only ones to be disappointed by the circumstances in which they found

UNITED EMPIRE LOYALISTS

Blacks entered Canada as servants to their White masters and as veterans who had gained their freedom by serving the British side in roles such as spies, guides, dam and bridge builders. The Blacks fought with intensity because their freedom was at stake.

themselves. Many White Loyalists soon gave up and returned to the United States. Black people, however, did not have that option since it would mean risking re-enslavement. A solution for some was provided in 1791 by an English anti-slavery society: free passage to Africa. In January 1791 a group of about 1,200 Black men, women and children sailed out of Halifax, bound for Sierra Leone.

The Maroons
A second wave of Black immigration occurred when hundreds of Black Jamaicans came to Halifax. They were the Maroons, descendants of runaway slaves who had lived for generations in the hills of Jamaica and fought fiercely to avoid being captured.

In 1796, British officials in Jamaica managed to trick some of the Maroons into surrendering. Then they put them on ships and sent them to Halifax. There the Maroons helped build the Halifax Citadel and even put their fighting experience to good use by forming a militia unit. But they didn't like the climate, and they didn't like Nova Scotia. Within four years most of the Maroons had sailed to Sierra Leone, the same country that Black Loyalists had sailed to a few years earlier.

> **SIERRA LEONE**
> Sierra Leone is a small country on the west coast of Africa, with Freetown as its capital. In 1787, Granville Sharp, a British abolitionist, established a colony as a home for over 2,000 freed slaves from Britain and the Americas at Freetown. The population was increased by the emancipation of Africans freed from slave ships. Sierra Leone was under British control from 1787 until 1961, when it became an independent country.

The War of 1812
In 1812, war broke out again between Britain and the United States, and this time much of the fighting was done on Canadian soil, especially in Upper Canada. Many African-Canadians fought for the British, and some of them joined a special military unit for Blacks, called Captain Runchey's Company of Coloured Men. The unit took part in the many border skirmishes and several major battles, including the war's most famous one, the Battle of Queenston Heights.

> During the War of 1812, Black volunteers fought and distinguished themselves at Queenston Heights, Fort George, Niagara Town, Stoney Creek, Lundy's Lane and other border skirmishes.
> Following the war, Sir Peregrine Maitland, Lieutenant-Governor of Upper Canada, offered Black veterans grants of land in what was to become the Township of Oro, near Barrie, Ontario.

In the United States, thousands of slaves escaped to fight for the British, who promised them freedom. After the war, about 2,000 of them came to Canada as refugees seeking protection from American slavery, and settled in Nova Scotia and New Brunswick.

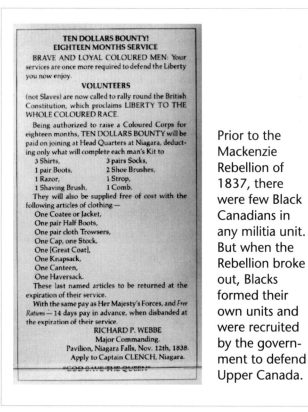

TEN DOLLARS BOUNTY!
EIGHTEEN MONTHS SERVICE

BRAVE AND LOYAL COLOURED MEN: Your services are once more required to defend the Liberty you now enjoy.

VOLUNTEERS

(not Slaves) are now called to rally round the British Constitution, which proclaims LIBERTY TO THE WHOLE COLOURED RACE.

Being authorized to raise a Coloured Corps for eighteen months, TEN DOLLARS BOUNTY will be paid on joining at Head Quarters at Niagara, deducting only what will complete each man's Kit to

3 Shirts,	3 pairs Socks,
1 pair Boots,	2 Shoe Brushes,
1 Razor,	1 Strop,
1 Shaving Brush,	1 Comb.

They will also be supplied free of cost with the following articles of clothing —
One Coatee or Jacket,
One pair Half Boots,
One pair cloth Trowsers,
One Cap, one Stock,
One [Great Coat],
One Knapsack,
One Canteen,
One Haversack.

These last named articles to be returned at the expiration of their service.

With the same pay as Her Majesty's Forces, and *Free Rations* — 14 days pay in advance, when disbanded at the expiration of their service.

RICHARD P. WEBBE
Major Commanding.
Pavilion, Niagara Falls, Nov. 12th, 1838.
Apply to Captain CLENCH, Niagara.

"GOD SAVE THE QUEEN"

Prior to the Mackenzie Rebellion of 1837, there were few Black Canadians in any militia unit. But when the Rebellion broke out, Blacks formed their own units and were recruited by the government to defend Upper Canada.

The Underground Railroad

In the late eighteenth century, a strong anti-slavery movement developed in the United States—but only in the northern states. Southerners remained convinced that their entire economy would collapse without slavery. One by one the northern states abolished slavery within their territory, but opposition from Southerners made it impossible to get a federal law passed abolishing it throughout the country. Moreover, pro-slavery forces managed in 1793 to get a law passed allowing slave owners to hunt down and retake runaway slaves who had escaped to free states. A later law, the Fugitive Slave Act of 1850, was even stronger. It decreed that anyone in the free states who had knowledge of runaway slaves was obliged to turn them in or face stiff penalties. These laws

Slaves were often auctioned to the highest bidder in the United States. Family members were often separated and sold to different owners.

meant that there was no real safety for escaped slaves anywhere within the United States.

After Governor Simcoe got his anti-slavery law passed in 1793, word spread that fugitive slaves would be free once they reached Upper Canada, and Black Americans began escaping north into the province. Later, with the complete abolition of slavery in Canada, the movement gained momentum. Most of the fugitives settled in southern Ontario, although some went to New Brunswick and Quebec.

Escaping was dangerous and difficult, especially for slaves from the Deep South. Canada and safety were a long way away. Many had to hide in woods and swamps, going days without food. They had to walk hundreds of kilometres, haunted every step by the

Fugitive slaves fleeing to escape slave hunters. *(Dramatization)*

THE UNDERGROUND RAILROAD

The Underground Railroad was used to refer to the passage of runaway slaves to Canada through the northern states. Assistance provided by Whites or free Blacks included transportation, hiding places and food. Most of the routes were secret trails. It was "underground" because it was secretive and not sponsored by any government.

Certain terms came into use that were common to railroad language, including the following:

Station: A safe place on the route north;

Freight or **Cargo**: Name given to runaway slaves;

Station Masters or Agents: Persons who would hide runaways and advise the slaves where to find the next safe station;

Conductors: Persons who accompanied slaves from one station to the next station.

Employees: Persons who assisted runaways. Quakers were very active in assisting slaves on their way to safety.

Stockholders: Persons who gave money to those assisting, such as boat operators, to purchase food and supplies.

Josiah Henson and the Dawn Settlement

Many Black Canadians have served as religious leaders over the years, but none has been as famous as Josiah Henson. Born into slavery in the United States in 1789, Henson later escaped with his wife and children to Canada, where he died many years later at the age of 94.

Henson had a miserable life as an American slave. His own father had been whipped and had his ear cut off and was sold to another slave owner while Josiah was still a boy. When he had grown into a man, Josiah Henson once helped his owner in a bar room fight. As a result, another White man later attacked Henson with a fence rail and broke his arm and shoulder blades. As a result, Henson was never able to straighten his arm properly again.

Henson was known to serve his slave-owners faithfully, and even to resist chances to run away. He became a Methodist Episcopal preacher in his spare time and saved his money in the hope of buying his freedom. Finally, however, after being cheated out of his savings by a slave owner, and after learning that he was to be sold to someone else, Henson escaped one night while his owner was away. Henson, who had been living in Kentucky, loaded his family onto a small boat and crossed the Ohio River. At the other side, in the State of Indiana, the Henson family walked at night, with the two youngest children in a pack on their father's back, and hid during the day. About six weeks later, after walking many miles and taking two ships, the Hensons arrived in Canada.

Josiah Henson and his wife.

At first, Henson worked as a farm labourer in southwestern Ontario. His son taught him to read, and Henson became a preacher for Blacks in the area. He also taught other Black farmers about the importance of owning their own land and growing a variety of products.

Henson returned to the United States to help many American slaves escape to Canada. He encouraged Blacks to be loyal to the British, and he lived by his word, fighting in support of the

Canadian government to put down the rebellion in Upper Canada in 1837-38.

THE DAWN SETTLEMENT

One of Henson's most important accomplishments was to help create a colony near Chatham, Ontario, where Blacks could study and live. Known as the Dawn Settlement, the colony was founded with the help of money raised partly by a sympathetic American Quaker named James Fuller.

At the heart of the Dawn Settlement was a school called the British American Institute. It was attended by children and adults, some of whom were Natives and Whites. The school began in the 1840s, and grew quickly.

The population of the Dawn Settlement grew to about 500 people. Some worked as farmers, and others worked in a sawmill, a gristmill and a brickyard. The settlement had many troubles, however. Henson and others involved with the project did not take good care of their money, and the settlement ended up owing a lot of money to other people. To make matters worse, some Blacks living nearby criticized the Dawn Settlement for encouraging Blacks to live apart from other people. The critics, who included the well-known newspaper editor Mary Ann Shadd, believed that Blacks would make more progress in society by living among, not apart from, other people.

The Dawn Settlement ended around 1872, but not before Josiah Henson had become quite famous. Years earlier, the story of his life appeared in a book called *The Life of Josiah Henson, Formerly a Slave, Now an Inhabitant of Canada*. After that, an American novel, *Uncle Tom's Cabin*, by Harriet Beecher Stowe, was published with great success. It told the story of an American slave named Tom who remained faithful to his slave-owners for many years before finally escaping to freedom. Many people came to believe, rightly or wrongly, that the book was about the life of Josiah Henson, and that made Henson even more famous.

Henson lived for many years in a small house in the Dawn Settlement, but he travelled widely in Canada, the United States and England, meeting people and giving speeches. When Henson died in 1883, people came to his funeral in 50 horse-drawn wagons. He had become a major figure during his life, and he had gone through some amazing changes, from slave to a world traveller and leader of his people.

fear of being recaptured. The odds against those who escaped on their own were enormous, and a great many were retaken and cruelly beaten.

Fortunately for many others, there were Americans and Canadians, both Black and White, who were willing to risk their own freedom and even their lives to help them.

By the time the second Fugitive Slave Act was passed, a network of escape routes, safe places and people willing to help was well established. It was known as the Underground Railroad, and the people who helped run it came from all possible walks of life. They were teachers and tavern keepers, housemaids and merchants. Many were members of a religious group called the Quakers, and many were former slaves who could not rest content as long as others remained in bondage.

Harriet Tubman was one of the most famous "conductors" of the Underground Railroad. Tubman had escaped American slavery as a young woman. She moved to St. Catharines, Ontario, in 1851. From there, she made 19

Fugitive slaves stopping at Levi and Catharine Coffin's to find shelter on their way to Canada. Levi Coffin, who was a Quaker, lived in Cincinnati, which was a major Underground Railroad station. He worked so hard at helping escaping slaves that he became known as the "President" of the Underground Railroad.

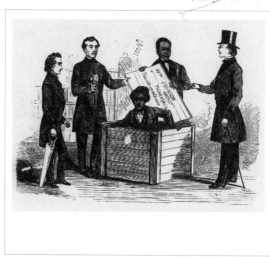

Slaves devised many innovative schemes to escape. One of the most daring was planned by Henry "Box" Brown, a slave from Richmond, Virginia, who had friends put him in a wooden crate and shipped to an Underground Railroad agent in Philadelphia.

secret trips into the United States to help fugitive slaves escape to Canada. Rewards totalling $40,000 were offered for her capture, but still she went, travelling by night, using the North Star to find her way. As an explanation for her willingness to take such risks, Tubman once told a writer simply, "I think slavery is the next thing to hell."

Another important conductor was Alexander Ross of Belleville, Ontario. Ross was a doctor, whose hobby was ornithology—the study of birds. He often travelled to slave plantations in the United States, pretending that he was there to study the bird life, but secretly helping slaves plan their escapes. Sometimes he guided the fugitives personally all the way to Canada.

The American Civil War

In some ways, the Fugitive Slave Law of 1850 backfired. Many Americans in the northern states had never given much thought to the issue of slavery. Now they found themselves cast in the role of slave catchers, and a lot of them didn't like it. Anti-slavery, or abolition, groups gained strength and, in some cases, became more aggressive. In 1858, an ardent abolitionist named John Brown planned an attack on an arsenal in Harpers Ferry, West Virginia. The idea was to take the stored weapons and use them to destroy slavery in the United States. Brown did much of his planning in Chatham, Ontario, and when the attack finally was launched in the fall of 1859, two Canadians took part. The attack failed and most of the participants, including Stewart Taylor, one of the Canadians, were killed in the raid or hanged later. However, the other Canadian, a Black man named Osborne Anderson, escaped back to Canada and later wrote a pamphlet about the raid.

A year and a half after Harpers Ferry, Americans were locked in a devastating civil war that pitted the slave-owning southern states against the northern states and the federal government. Slavery was only one of the issues, but to Black people across the continent, it was the over-riding one. Osborne Anderson returned to the United States to help the Union army against the rebellious southern states. So did other African-Canadians, including Anderson Ruffin Abbott, the first Black doctor born in Canada, and Mary Ann Shadd, a well-known teacher and newspaper

Harriet Tubman

John Brown came to Canada to plan his attack on Harpers Ferry, West Virginia, to overthrow the American government and with it slavery. The attack failed and Brown was hanged on December 2, 1859.

Page 26

An American ship captain sailed his boat into Canadian waters in September of 1860, with an American slave on board. The slave, a young boy named Charles Mitchell, had stowed away on the ship when it left the United States. The captain found him and planned to take him back to his slave master. However, while the ship was in harbour at Victoria, British Columbia, local Blacks learned that Charles was locked up in a cabin. A Victoria sheriff removed the boy from the boat, over the loud the protests of the ship's captain. Soon after, a judge ruled that the boy had to be set free. Charles Mitchell stayed in Canada and went to school in Victoria.

publisher. Harriet Tubman went too, and served as a nurse, guide and spy for the Union army. In 1863, before the war ended, the American President, Abraham Lincoln, issued the Emancipation Proclamation that declared that "all persons held as slaves" in the rebellious southern states would be "thenceforward and forever free."

After the Union Army won the Civil War in 1865, a constitutional amendment confirmed the end of slavery in the United States. American Blacks no longer needed to flee to Canada to escape slavery, and, in fact, many Blacks who had come earlier now returned to the United States.

The Canadian West

The first big movement of Blacks into western Canada took place shortly before the Civil War, when a group of Black

Osborne Perry Anderson

Sylvia and Louis Stark came to British Columbia with a group of about 600 California Blacks in 1858. Many of the Blacks stayed in Victoria and others settled elsewhere on Vancouver Island, but the Starks joined a group of pioneer Blacks, Whites and Polynesians who moved to Saltspring Island to live off the land. Life on the island proved difficult and rugged. On the day they arrived, the Starks witnessed a battle between Haida and Cowichan Indians, and they moved into a log cabin with no roof or door. The Starks had two children at the time, and they were expecting a third child. They used oxen to pull tree stumps from the ground, and grew fruit trees, vegetables and wheat. They also raised chickens, turkeys, pigs and cows, but that created problems too, because bears sometimes killed the pigs.

Although the land was rich and the winter climate among the mildest in Canada, the Starks and other settlers still had to deal with problems they could not prevent or avoid. During one cold winter, more than 100 cattle starved to death on the island. The next year, people living on the island and in other parts of British Columbia suffered terribly from a smallpox epidemic, which killed thousands of Indian people. Louis Stark and his family were vaccinated against the disease, but the vaccination itself made Louis very ill. He recovered, fortunately, and his family stayed on Saltspring Island for about 15 years before returning to live on Vancouver Island.

The Victoria Pioneer Rifle Company was a Black militia unit formed in Victoria in 1860. For a time it was the only organized defense force in Victoria.

Californians decided to move north. California was a free state, but Blacks faced many forms of discrimination there and had good reason to fear a Fugitive Slave Act that would not even allow their testimony to be heard should anyone claim they were fugitives. In 1858, about 600 Black Californians sailed to Victoria, on Vancouver Island. They settled there, on Saltspring Island and on the British Columbian mainland. The area was booming at the time. People were looking for gold, buying land, building houses and starting businesses. The Black immigrants got involved in every kind of work. Some became manual labourers, house servants and barbers. Others ran their own stores and restaurants. Several took on jobs as policemen in Victoria, later forming the first militia unit in what is now British Columbia. The all-Black unit, formed in 1860, was called the Victoria Pioneer Rifle Company, also known as the African Rifles. Mifflin Gibbs, one of the leaders of the Black community, built several businesses in Victoria, served on the City Council and later encouraged British Columbia to become part of Canada.

It would be several years yet before any sizeable number of Blacks would move to the Canadian prairies. One of the first and best-known to do so was John Ware, a Texas cowboy who arrived in what is now Alberta in 1882.

John Ware and his family, about 1896.

A tall and powerful man, Ware used guns and lassoes expertly, had great skill with horses and could handle the toughest ranch animals. As a matter of fact, he occasionally wrestled huge steers to the ground and won prize money in roping and riding competitions. Ware had been born a slave in the United States, and was freed when slavery ended in that country in 1865. After moving to Canada, he married a woman named Mildred Lewis, raised five children and died the way he lived—riding a horse. His death, in 1905, occurred when his horse stepped in a hole, fell heavily to the ground and landed on him.

A few years after Ware died, 1000 or so Black American farmers moved north to settle in Manitoba, Saskatchewan and Alberta. Most of them came from Oklahoma, which passed a number of discriminatory laws after becoming a state in 1907. Many homesteaded successfully in Canada but others found the blossoming cities more to their taste. By 1911, there were about 150 Blacks living in Winnipeg, roughly the same number in Vancouver and nearly 300 in Edmonton.

Closing the Door

In 1911, word spread that large numbers of Black Oklahomans were getting ready to take up the Canadian

Mattie Mayes was born in slavery, about 1850, on a Georgia plantation. She married Joe Mayes, who was a pastor, and they moved to Oklahoma. They learned of opportunities in Saskatchewan and in 1910 they came to Canada with others from Oklahoma and settled in a community about 30 kilometres from North Battleford to homestead. Joe became the first pastor of the congregation, and in 1916 the Shiloh Baptist Church was founded, near Maidstone. By 1920 the Oklahoma colony was well established. Over the years, Mattie earned admiration in the community for her warmth and caring. Later in life, she moved to Edmonton, where she died in 1953. In 1971, in the yard of the Shiloh Baptist Church, a memorial plaque was dedicated to Mattie Mayes and her family.

government's offer of virtually free land in Western Canada. Many Canadians got very upset at the idea of a massive influx of Black immigrants. In response to their protests, the government devised ways to keep Black immigrants out. Immigration regulations did not openly discriminate on the basis or race or colour, but officials were instructed to reject Black immigrants on medical grounds.

About 20,000 Blacks lived in Canada in 1921. Most of them had been born in Canada. Of those who had been born elsewhere, most came from the United States. That situation stayed basically the same until after the end of the Second World War.

Reverend William King

The Elgin Settlement

The most successful and best known of the early Black communities in Ontario was probably the Elgin Settlement, which was the idea of Reverend William King, a White Presbyterian minister who was born in Ireland in 1812. As a young man, King moved to the United States and married an American woman. He came to work as a missionary in Canada West, as Ontario was then called, in 1846. When his father- in-law died and left him 14 American slaves in his will, King, an active abolitionist, found himself in a very embarrassing position. He went south to meet the slaves in Ohio, set them free and offered them the chance to live in a settlement that he planned to build in Canada. They accepted his offer and settled near Chatham in 1848.

Some White people in the area protested strongly, but King and the former slaves created the Elgin Settlement in November 1849. King formed a group that sold land to Black setters at a low price. In exchange, the settlers were required to clear their fields, build houses, dig irrigation ditches and build up the community in general. By 1854, about 300 Black families had moved into the settlement.

The Elgin Settlement grew into a successful community. People farmed the land and worked on the railways; carpenters and shoemakers opened shops; a brickmaker set up business; schools and churches were built. Over time the settlers gained the acceptance of neighbouring White communities.

Some of the Black settlers in the Elgin Settlement returned to the United States after the Civil War. But the

With his wife and four children, Isaac Riley was the first to purchase land and settle in the Elgin Settlement in November, 1849.

settlement survived, and many Blacks still live in the area, which is now known as Buxton.

Africville

Nova Scotia was the first area in Canada to form important Black communities, and one of its best known was Africville.

Africville, in the north end of Halifax, existed for more than 100 years before it was destroyed in the 1960s. Its first settlers were Blacks who had come from other parts of Nova Scotia, such as Preston and Hammonds Plains, to find work in Halifax. In 1851, just over 54 Blacks lived in Africville, but the population had grown to more than 400 a century later. One of its most important features was its Baptist church, which had also served as a school in the early years.

Africville

In the 1960s people of Africville owned land, houses and businesses, but they had serious problems to contend with. Although they paid taxes, the city did not provide proper water, sewage and police services. Factories, a prison and a garbage dump had been located close to the community, and railway tracks ran through the middle of it.

The residents of Africville wanted to stay where they were and they wanted the city of Halifax to provide the services they needed and deserved. Instead, the city insisted that the community be destroyed and its people relocated in public housing. It humiliated them by using garbage trucks to move them and their belongings out. The last home in Africville, which belonged to a 72-year-old man named Aaron Carvery, was destroyed in 1970. But Africville lives on in the minds of Black Nova Scotians. Every year, former residents gather to remember the Africville community.

CHAPTER FIVE

Black Churches and Schools

Churches and schools formed the heart of Black communities in early Canada. When they were not allowed to attend those that served other Canadians, as happened all too often, Black people founded their own schools and taught at them, built their own churches and became ministers, deacons and elders for their people.

It was not until Blacks had the right to take part in a wide range of community life—especially the schools—that they could even begin to enjoy equal treatment in society. However, one benefit that came out of having to attend separate schools and churches is that Black Canadians developed a strong sense of identity in their own communities.

Churches

Some early Canadian churches created separate places where Blacks had to worship, apart from others. Other churches didn't let Blacks in at all. In their own churches, Blacks had the freedom to get together, to create their own values, to plan events and, basically, to control their own lives more than they could in the outside world. As a result,

Chapel at Uncle Tom's Cabin site at Dresden, Ontario

the Black church often became much more than a place of worship. It became a place where people met, where leaders developed skills and where members discussed community issues.

Many types of Black churches were created in early Canada. The most common denominations were Baptist, African Methodist Episcopal and British Methodist Episcopal.

The Nova Scotia Experience

Nova Scotia has some of the oldest Black settlements in the country, and the history of its Baptist churches tells us a lot about the trials Blacks faced and the triumphs they enjoyed in their early years in Canada.

In Nova Scotia, as in other parts of the country, the church became a kind of second home to Black people—a home they could take charge of with dignity and pride.

In the late 1700s, when Black Loyalists who left the American colonies to settle in Nova Scotia, they had no choice but to live in segregated settlements and form their own churches and schools. A few years later, when over a third of them left Nova Scotia for Africa, many of the leaders of the Black Community, including teachers and preachers, went with them, leaving the remaining community weakened.

Around that time, a White missionary named John Burton began to work with the Black community in Halifax. He founded the First Baptist Church and had a congregation of some 30 members, which grew to 300 within 20 years. Burton's church was poor as neither he himself nor his members had much money. Still they survived.

Burton worked hard for the Black community, ignoring warnings from some prejudiced White missionaries not to socialize with the Black people, or to eat or sleep in their homes, or to let untrained Blacks do any preaching. In 1816, he began to help a young Black man named Richard Preston, who would become one of the most important church and community leaders in Nova Scotia.

Preston had escaped slavery in the United States and had come to Nova Scotia in search of his mother, whom he found in the town that carried his last name. Preston arrived in Halifax at a time when many Nova Scotians op-

Richard Preston, who escaped slavery in Virginia, arrived in Nova Scotia in 1816. He became an ordained Baptist minister and a leader in both the church and the community, helping to found the African Baptist Church in Halifax and the African United Baptist Association.

posed the admission of Black immigrants. He was welcomed, however, by John Burton who set him to work as a preacher for the Baptist Church in Black communities outside Halifax.

Preston had a good sense of humour and spoke well, and within a few years he was known in all the Black communities in Nova Scotia. He believed that it was important for Black and White people to work together. Nevertheless, from his earliest years in the province, he could see that many White Nova Scotians refused to accept Blacks as their equals. When he became the first Black person to join a Baptists' club called the Maritime Baptist Association, for instance, some members opposed him because of his race.

There were other examples too. In 1825, after a disagreement among members of the Anglican Church in Halifax, several White members decided to leave. They joined John Burton's First Baptist Church, but they soon left it too because they didn't like going to church with Blacks. They ended up forming their own church, called the Second Baptist Church.

Blacks owned and controlled the Cornwallis Street Baptist Church, founded in Halifax, Nova Scotia, in 1832. Richard Preston was its first minister.

A few years later, Richard Preston left for England to be trained as a Baptist minister. There he completed his formal training and was ordained. He also joined the movement to abolish slavery, gave public lectures and raised enough money to build a new Baptist church upon his return to Halifax. It was called the Cornwallis Street African Baptist Church, and he served as its first minister.

Over the next twenty years, Preston helped set up 11 Baptist churches and established himself as a community leader known all over the province. He encouraged church members to press for changes that would make life easier for Blacks in Nova Scotia and used the church to emphasize that Blacks needed jobs, land and education. Perhaps Preston's most important accomplishment was the creation, in 1854, of the African United Baptist Association. The Association, made up of representatives from the 12 Black Baptist churches in Nova Scotia at the time, went on to become one of the most important Black associations in the history of Nova Scotia. It struggled to improve schools for Black children, helped create a home for Black orphans, and has continued serving the Black community right up to modern times.

Schools

Education has always been important to Blacks in Canada. Education, they knew, would help them find jobs, gain standing in the larger community and give their children a good start in life.

However, many of Canada's earliest towns and villages had no public schools at all. And some communities that did have schools refused to let Black children attend. In the mid-1800s, laws were passed in Nova Scotia and Ontario to keep Black children in separate schools. As a result, Blacks had no choice but to arrange their own education. Through religious and other groups, sometimes on their own and at other times with help from the outside community, African-Canadians worked hard to provide an education for their children.

One of the earliest examples of classroom education for Black children goes back to a time when many children, White or Black, had no schooling at all. More than 200 years ago in Nova Scotia, a group of White people connected with the Church of England paid teachers and bought books so that the children of some Black Loyalists could go to school. The children were educated by Black teachers such as Joseph Leonard, who gave lessons in his home in Brindley Town, and Catherine Abernathy, who taught in a log schoolhouse built by Black residents in Preston. More schools of the same kind opened in other Nova Scotian towns.

Soon afterwards, education for Blacks began in New Brunswick. Again with help

> Arthur Richardson was the first Black man to go to university in New Brunswick. Richardson, who had lived in Bermuda before coming to Saint John, graduated from the University of New Brunswick in 1833. Mary Matilda Winslow, of Woodstock, completed her studies at the same university in 1905. Neither Richardson nor Winslow was able to find a teaching position in New Brunswick. Both found work in other provinces and then taught in the United States, where it was not as difficult for educated Blacks to get a good job.

This picture of the school children and their teacher, George Cromwell was taken about 1910 at North Buxton, Ontario.

from the Church of England, a school for Black children was set up in Fredericton. The African School in Saint John was that city's first school for Black residents, and it remained in use for nearly 20 years. In the last half of the 1800s, Black students in Charlottetown, Prince Edward Island, attended the Old Bog School, which was also attended by White people.

Some of the schools created for Black children were of very good quality. One example was the Buxton Mission School in Ontario. It opened its doors in 1850 to serve the new Black settlement in Elgin. The school had excellent teachers, and it was soon considered better than other schools in the area. As a result, White parents started sending their children to Buxton too. Before long, Whites made up about half of the student population. The school lasted for 15 years, giving a fine education to hundreds of children and to many adults. Finally, however, many Black families left the region after the American Civil War and the school became part of the local school system.

The Buxton school worked out well, but as time went on African-Canadian parents objected strongly to having to send their children to schools just for Black students. Most of these schools were under-funded, poorly equipped and inadequately staffed. Black parents wanted their children to have the same educational opportunities as everybody else, and they tried harder and harder to have all public schools open to all children. It was a long struggle. Segregation continued until 1954 in Nova Scotia and 1964 in Ontario.

In Ontario, the law that permitted school segregation was finally changed after politicians heard a strong protest from Leonard Braithwaite, a lawyer, who was the first Black elected to a Canadian Parliament. In his first speech to the Ontario Legislature, Braithwaite spoke out strongly against Ontario schools that were still keeping Black children apart from White.

Because of the efforts of people like Leonard Braithwaite, it is now against the law for schools to keep out students because of their race. Today, Blacks, like children of every other race and ethnic background, study in schools and universities from coast to coast. Many become teachers, principals and school or university administrators.

One of the best known Black teachers in early Ontario was Mary Ann Shadd. Working out of Windsor in the mid-1800s, a time when Blacks were not allowed to attend public schools in town, Mary Ann Shadd ran a private school for Black students. Her salary was paid partly by parents and partly by donations from the American Missionary Association. Her students ranged from age four to 45, and her classes included geography, history, arithmetic, grammar, reading and botany. Highly respected for her teaching skills, Mary Ann Shadd later became known as a newspaper editor and for fighting against slavery during the American Civil War. Today, a public school in Scarborough, Ontario, bears her name.

Wilson O. Brooks was the first Black school principal in Toronto, and possibly the city's first Black teacher too. He began teaching in 1952 at the Brock Avenue Public School. He served as a principal from 1966 to 1986 at various schools, including the Shaw Junior Public School and the Glen Ames Senior Public School. Brooks, who was born in Windsor, was also one of the first Black commissioned officers in the Royal Canadian Air Force to serve in a bomber squadron during the Second World War. He became an officer in 1944, at the age of 19, and rose to the rank of flying officer. In the Air Force, as a teacher and as a principal, Brooks was a pioneer. He made it easier for African-Canadians to find work in areas that they had been kept out of previously.

Heritage programs now exist in schools and community centres across the country to teach children about the history and contribution of African-Canadians. Black parents, educators and community leaders are working hard, often with help from the wider community, to make sure that schools give their children a good education.

Leonard Braithwaite, a lawyer living in Etobicoke, Ontario, was the first Black elected to a Canadian Parliament. He served as a Liberal Member of the Ontario Provincial Legislature from 1963 until 1975. In his first speech to the Ontario Legislature, Braithwaite spoke out strongly against some Ontario schools that were still keeping Black children apart from Whites. After Braithwaite's criticism, the Ontario government got rid of a law that had allowed for school segregation.

The Garvey Institute school in Montreal appears to be Canada's only private school created to meet the needs of the Black community. Founded in 1983 in the Little Burgundy neighbourhood in downtown Montreal, the school has about 40 students from kindergarten to grade 6. The school is named after Marcus Garvey, the famous Jamaican who encouraged Blacks around the world to be proud of themselves. In 1990, students from the Garvey Institute sang the international African Anthem,"Nkosi Sikeleli Afrika", to Winnie and Nelson Mandela, who were visiting from South Africa.

CHAPTER SIX

Caribbean People in Canada

The Caribbean is a chain of islands that lie in the Atlantic Ocean between North and South America. Like Canada, the Caribbean has been populated by people from all over the world. A few are of Aboriginal, and some are of Asian, European or mixed racial background. A great many are of African ancestry because the Caribbean islands were the biggest market in the Atlantic slave trade. It is estimated that almost half the slaves shipped from Africa were destined for the Caribbean.

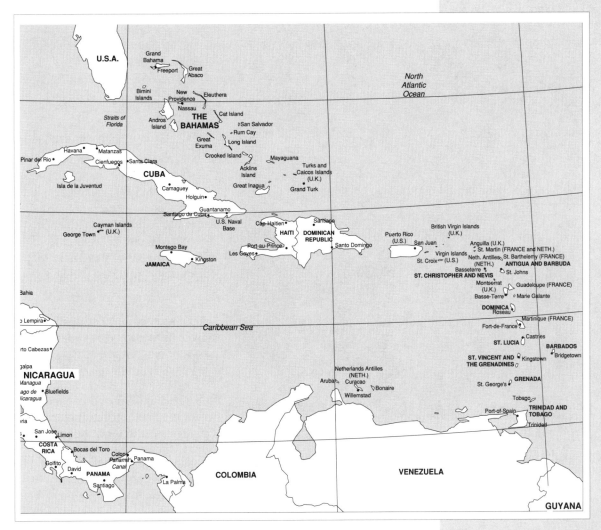

After slavery ended in the Caribbean, it became common for people to move in search of better jobs or better farming land. Many Caribbean people left their countries, found work elsewhere and sent money back home to help their families, a practice that continues to this day.

Today, most of the more than 350,000 Blacks who live in Canada are of Caribbean background. And most of them have come since the 1960s. Other than the Maroons, who didn't stay, only a handful of Caribbean immigrants came to Canada before the 1900s, settling in places such as Nova Scotia, Ontario and British Columbia. Around the turn of the twentieth century, some men were brought from Caribbean islands, such as Barbados, to work in coal mines near Sydney, Nova Scotia.

Many Caribbean people wanted to come to Canada in the first half of the 1900s. Seeking better jobs in order to help their families and improve their lives, hundred of thousands went to Britain and the United States. Canada needed more workers at the time and was inviting immigrants to come from Europe and the United States, but Canadian immigration policy discriminated against Blacks and other people of colour.

It was not until the 1960s did that the government make it easier for Blacks and other racial minorities, such as Asians and South Asian people, to come to Canada. Rules were

Thousands of people sing, dance, eat and meet at Caribana every August in Toronto. It is Canada's biggest cultural festival. A highlight of the two-week celebration is the Caribana parade with participants dressed in lavish costumes, such as this woman. Such celebrations are held in other cities across as well.

changed at that time so that education and needed job skills became the main criteria for accepting would-be immigrants. Caribbean people were suddenly able to come in large numbers — and each year thousands did, especially from Jamaica, Guyana, Trinidad and Tobago, Haiti and Barbados. In the 1970s, more than 200,000 people came to Canada from the Caribbean; in the 1980s, more than 84,000.

Unlike earlier Black immigrants, those from the Caribbean have settled overwhelmingly in the cities, and especially in the Toronto area. However, many Haitians, who speak French, have preferred to live in Montreal, which now has a large Haitian community.

It has not been easy for Caribbean immigrants to adjust to Canada. Coming from a tropical climate, some have difficulty getting used to Canadian winters. For many, the loneliness of moving to a new country has been even harder than the climate. Often, men came alone and brought their families much later. Women too came alone to work as domestics because for a time this was one of the few ways that Caribbean people were allowed to come to Canada. Many of these women had very good job skills, and had worked as nurses or teachers in their home countries, but they gave it all up to start a new life as domestics in Canada.

After arriving in Canada, some Blacks of Caribbean ancestry have been refused jobs and places to live, just because of the colour of their skin. Others have found it hard to get used to new customs, new schools and new ways of speaking.

The chart to the right shows, as of 1991, the number of people living in Canada who were born in the Caribbean, Bermuda, Guyana and Africa.

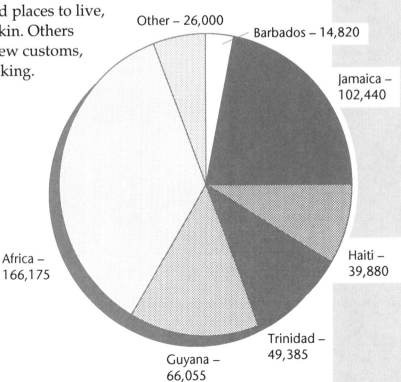

Other – 26,000
Barbados – 14,820
Jamaica – 102,440
Haiti – 39,880
Trinidad – 49,385
Guyana – 66,055
Africa – 166,175

To this day, some Blacks of Caribbean and other origins continue to find difficulties in Canada. Some of their greatest problems have to do with not being encouraged to do well in school, not having opportunities to find jobs that make use of their working skills, and sometimes not being able to find any job. However, many other Blacks have overcome these difficulties and built good lives here. Many have excelled in schools, at university and at work. They have started newspapers and magazines, written books, formed businesses, entered politics, joined trades and professions.

CHAPTER SEVEN

Black Contributions in Canada

For many years, most African-Canadians had little choice but to work in hard jobs that did not pay well. They often had the skills and knowledge to do other work, but employers would not hire them—at least not if White people were available. Women mainly worked as house cleaners, nannies, in laundries and in restaurants. Men, on the whole, were limited to working as hotel doormen, janitors, barbers, shoe shiners, bell hops and railway porters. Even when at war for Canada, Black men were often given only the worst jobs.

Considering how few choices Blacks once had in the Canadian working world, it is amazing how far they have come.

Politics

During their many years as slaves in Canada and the United States, Blacks had no political rights. They could not vote, and of course, they could not serve as politicians because they were not considered to be full members of society. Even after slavery ended, a long time passed before Blacks had the same rights as other people. Perhaps because they or their ancestors have been denied such rights in the past, African-Canadians have long recognized that getting involved in politics is an important way to take part in society and to help make it better. From the east coast of Canada to the west, Blacks have found many ways to play a role in politics.

One of the earliest Black politicians in Canadian history was Mifflin Wistar Gibbs, who came to Victoria in 1858. Gibbs was an educated man who had run a successful business selling shoes and clothes in California. When he arrived in Victoria, he set up a new business selling groceries and supplies to gold miners, and settled in a wealthy part of Victoria. Gibbs knew a great deal about the history of Black people, and he became a natural leader of the new

Black community in Victoria. In 1866, he was elected to the city council, and the next year he ran the committee in charge of Victoria's financial affairs. Gibbs also played a role in encouraging British Columbia to become part of Canada, which it did in 1871. Gibbs returned to the United States to become a judge and, later, a representative of the United States government in the African country of Madagascar.

Alfred Shadd was the first Black Canadian to run in a provincial election. Shadd was born in Ontario in 1870. As a young man, he moved to the North-West Territories in search of adventure. At the age of 26, Shadd arrived in the town of Kinistino to work as a teacher. A little girl, who had never seen a Black person before, sat on his knee and tried to rub the colour off his cheek. He smiled and let her know that his colour was there to stay.

Shadd, too, was there to stay, spending most of the rest of his life in the area. In 1901, he tried but failed to get elected as a Conservative member of the North-West Territories Assembly. Four years later, when part of the Territories became the province of Saskatchewan, Shadd ran again for political office. Again he was defeated, losing by just 52 votes to a Liberal friend named Thomas Sanderson.

Although he failed to become a provincial politician, Shadd remained an active member of the community. He worked as a teacher, and later as a doctor and a farmer. As well, he wrote for and owned a local newspaper, owned a drugstore and was an active member of the All Saints Anglican Church. Trained in medicine at the University of Toronto, Shadd travelled long distances in all kinds of weather to treat his patients. On one visit, he delivered a baby boy in a family's farmhouse and a calf in its barn.

Known as Doc Shadd, and admired for his hard work and his great sense of humour, Alfred Shadd died in 1915, leaving the people of Melfort, Saskatchewan, with a great sense of loss. At his funeral, the church overflowed with even more people standing outside than were seated inside, and his funeral procession was more than three kilometres long.

William Peyton Hubbard was born in Toronto in 1842, and became a well-known politician in the city around the turn of the century. Before entering politics, Hubbard

William Hubbard

worked for many years as a baker, and also worked driving horse-drawn cabs. One winter day, while he was driving on Don Mills Road in Toronto, he came across an accident in which a man in another cab was in danger of falling into the icy waters of the Don River. Hubbard rescued the man, who turned out to be George Brown, the well-known publisher of the Globe and one of Canada's Fathers of Confederation. Hubbard became Brown's personal driver, as well as his friend. Brown encouraged Hubbard to go into politics.

Hubbard served as a City of Toronto alderman from 1894 to 1907, and again in 1913. Sometimes he took on the job of acting mayor. He was known for his great debating skills, and for helping people who had little power in society. While in politics, he helped protect Chinese laundry owners from being driven out of business by richer competitors.

Hubbard died at the age of 93, and his descendants still live in Ontario.

A number of Blacks have served in city politics in Nova Scotia. Since the late 1800s, voters in the Preston area have steadily elected Blacks as councillors in Halifax County. Blacks have also been elected to municipal council in areas such as Halifax, Amherst and New Glasgow.

Daurene Lewis is a seventh generation Nova Scotian and members of her family have lived in Annapolis Royal since 1783. She is a descendent of Rose Fortune, who, as Canada's first police woman, worked in the port of Annapolis Royal in the late 1700s and early 1800s. Lewis graduated from Dalhousie University and taught nursing in Nova Scotia and Ontario. From 1984 to 1988, Lewis served as mayor of Annapolis Royal. She was the first Black mayor in the province, and the first Black woman mayor in Canada.

It was not until 1963, when Leonard Braithwaite was elected to the Ontario Legislature, that Blacks finally began to succeed in provincial and federal politics. He served as

> Howard McCurdy, born in 1932 in London, Ontario, holds a PhD. in microbiology and chemistry from Michigan State University. In 1959, McCurdy began teaching science at the University of Windsor. Later, he became the head of its biology department. McCurdy has volunteered his time and skills for more than 30 years in the field of human rights. That has involved making sure that Blacks have the basic opportunities that all Canadians want to enjoy, such as the right to go to school, to have a place to live, to work and to be served in stores, offices and restaurants. McCurdy served for several years as an alderman on the Windsor City Council. Since 1984, he has been the Member of Parliament for the riding of Windsor-St. Clair, Ontario.

Daurene Lewis

The Honourable
Lincoln Alexander

the Liberal member for Etobicoke for 12 years. Braithwaite, who is a lawyer, graduated from Osgoode Hall Law School and from the Harvard University School of Business Administration.

In 1968, Lincoln Alexander became the first Black elected to the House of Commons. Alexander, born in Toronto in 1922, served as the Progressive Conservative Member for Hamilton West until 1979. In his final year in Parliament, he was the federal Minister of Labour, marking the first time a Black had been a Cabinet Minister of any Canadian government. Alexander made history again in 1985 when he became the first Black lieutenant-governor. He served Ontario in that capacity until 1991.

In 1972, Rosemary Brown became the first Black woman elected to a provincial legislature. She served as a New Democratic Party Member of the British Columbia government. Brown, who was born in Jamaica and came to Canada in 1950, remained a member of the B.C. legislature until 1986.

In 1984, Anne Cools became the first Black appointed to the Canadian Senate. Cools, who was born in Barbados, was a social worker before entering politics.

Emery Barnes was first elected to the British Columbia legislature in 1972. He was re-elected for the fifth time in 1991, making him the longest-serving member of the Legislative Assembly. He has been appointed Deputy Speaker of the Legislature. Barnes, who was born in New Orleans, studied at the University of Oregon before moving to Canada. Barnes was a well-known athlete long before entering politics. He was an Olympic high jumper in 1952. Later he played professional football with the Green Bay Packers of the NFL before joining the BC Lions.

The Media

Blacks were publishing newspapers before Confederation created the Dominion of Canada in 1867.

One of the earliest papers was the *Provincial Freeman*, which Mary Ann Shadd published in Ontario (which was called Canada West at the time) between 1853 and 1858. Shadd, the first woman in North America to start a newspaper and edit it, worked with her brother Isaac on the *Provincial Freeman*. The *Freeman* called for an end to slavery in the United States and other mistreatment of Blacks.

From 1851 to about 1853, Henry Bibb published another Black paper called *The Voice of the Fugitive*. It was published out of Sandwich and Windsor, Ontario and was aimed at Blacks who had escaped slavery in the United States.

The *Voice of the Fugitive* was owned and edited by Henry Bibb. The paper provided information that was helpful to Blacks who had just come to Canada, escaping slavery in the United States.

The *Provincial Freeman* was founded by The Reverend Samuel Ringgold Ward, appearing on March 25, 1853. A Presbyterian minister, Ward organized branches of the Anti-Slavery Society throughout Canada West. Ward was highly regarded as an outstanding orator and newspaperman. As its first full-time editor, Mary Ann Shadd became the first Black newspaperwoman in Canada. The *Freeman* urged Blacks to become educated and self-reliant, and also pointed out instances of discrimination against Blacks.

An interesting publication in the early 1900s was the monthly magazine *Neith*. Published in Saint John, New Brunswick, it was founded by A. B. Walker, a barrister who had been born in British Columbia. *Neith* lasted on a year or so, but it was a lively, well-written magazine that was as good as or better than other publications at that time.

The *Free Lance*, which called itself "Canada's Greatest Negro Weekly," was published in Montreal from 1934 to 1941. A few years later, in 1946, Carrie Best of New Glasgow, Nova Scotia, began publishing *The Clarion*, which for a time was called *The Negro Citizen*. For ten years Best used the newspaper to let people know about restaurants and theatres that refused to serve Blacks, and to share information about people and events in the Black community.

Today, Blacks continue to publish newspapers and

magazines such as the *Provincial Monitor* in Halifax, *Share* in Toronto, and the *Afro-Canadian* in Montreal. *Caribe*, a Winnipeg-based magazine that took a special interest in books and in Black history, published its final issue in December 1990. It had been in business since 1979.

Some of Canada's best-known Black media personalities include CBC television journalists Hamlin Grange and Ona Fletcher. Cecil Foster writes for the Financial Post and is the author of the novel *No Man in the House*. African-Canadians work for newspapers and in television and radio stations in many parts of Canada.

The Arts

In North America, Blacks have always shown a strong interest in the arts. Under slavery, they were rarely allowed to gather in large groups, explore their interests, learn to read or develop their skills. After slavery ended, Blacks continued to find most doors closed to them when they looked for work, tried to study and wanted to take part in society. Telling stories, singing and dancing became important ways for Blacks to share their happiness and pain.

The simple act of storytelling is a basic human pleasure that has died out in many societies. In Black culture, it is a centuries-old tradition that remains very much alive. In many African societies, one of the most important members is the griot, or local storyteller. Griots are men or women who spend their lives learning about the people of their towns or villages—both living people and ancestors who died long ago. The traditional historians of African culture, they make their living by telling these stories, or singing them, at concerts, marriages, funerals and other gatherings. It is said that when a griot dies, so much knowledge is lost that it is as if a library burned down.

Africans transported as slaves to the Caribbean and North America brought this tradition of story telling with them. In Canada, Rita Cox is one of the leaders of the Canadian story telling community. Cox grew up in Trinidad in a culture where storytelling was part of everyday life. Adults told ghost stories, fables, tales about the dangers of life and fantasies about insects and animals with human qualities. Whenever stories were told, children were welcome to gather around and listen. When Cox came to Canada, she

Portia White was an internationally recognized contralto from Truro, Nova Scotia. She performed in several countries and was referred to as the "Marion Anderson of Canada".

brought her love of storytelling with her.

Before starting to tell a story, Cox traditionally says "Crick." The audience has to answer "Crack." Then she says, "Monkey break my back," and the story begins. She often ends each story by saying: "And I jump on the wire, and the wire bend, and that's the way my story end."

Cox tells stories in school classrooms, takes part in storytelling festivals and has started the Storytellers' School of Toronto, which holds courses and other activities each year for people who like to tell stories. She is also involved in Story Fast, an annual event in which Toronto school children gather to tell their own stories.

As head of Parkdale Public Library in Toronto, Cox has built up a collection of more than 2,500 books about Blacks. She has received numerous awards and honours, including the Governor General's Commemorative Medal for her significant contribution to Canada to celebrate Canada's 125th anniversary in 1992.

Rita Cox

Canada's most famous jazz musician is pianist Oscar Peterson, who was born in Montreal in 1925. Peterson was well known in his hometown and in jazz circles across Canada by the time he was 20, but his international reputation took off when he played at Carnegie Hall in New York when he was 24. Since then, he has delighted audiences around the world with his keyboard artistry, and he has also achieved recognition for his work as a composer. He has received Juno, Grammy and numerous other awards, and has been named a Companion of the Order of Canada.

Singer-songwriter Dan Hill was the first Black Canadian to achieve major international success in pop music. His single "Sometimes When We Touch" came out in 1977 and sold millions of copies around the world. Hill was born in 1954 in Toronto and put out his tenth album "Dance of Love" in 1991.

Oscar Peterson

Dan Hill

In the early 1990s, Michie Mee was a growing name in the Canadian rap scene. Born in Kingston, Jamaica, she moved to Toronto at the age of seven. In 1992, Atlantic Records released her album *Jamaican Funk – Canadian Style*. Michie Mee has performed with the deejay l.a.luv, mixing rap and reggae sounds.

Austin Clarke is one of Canada's best-known novelists. He was born in Barbados in 1934 and came to Canada as a student in 1955. Among his many works is a trilogy about the lives of Caribbean immigrants in Toronto. The novels making up the trilogy are *The Meeting Point*, *Storm of Fortune* and *The Bigger Light*.

Michie Mee and l.a.luv

Maestro Fresh-Wes was the first Canadian rap artist to achieve major success. He was born of Guyanese parents in Toronto in 1968. His first LP, "Symphony In Effect", sold more than 150,000 copies in Canada. In 1991, Maestro Fresh-Wes won the first Canadian Juno Award for the "best rap recording" category. In his second LP, "Black Tie Affair", Maestro Fresh-Wes raps on topics such as Black poetry and the Black Canadian identity.

Lillian Allen, a Toronto poet of Jamaican origin, performs what is called dub poetry, which is poetry set to music. She has won Juno Awards for her albums *Revolutionary Tea Party* and *Conditions Critical*. She has also produced a tape of dub poetry for children called *If You See Truth*.

Austin Clarke

John Alleyne

Over the years, Canadian ballet companies have featured a number of Black dancers, the best known of whom is probably John Alleyne. Born in Barbados, Alleyne graduated in 1978 from Canada's National Ballet School. He joined the National Ballet of Canada in 1984, working as a solo dancer and later as a choreographer whose work combines powerful movements with equally strong emotions. Alleyne has acquired an international reputation for his work, which has been performed in Canada, the United States and Germany. In 1990, he won the award for Best Choreographer at the International Ballet Competition in Jackson, Mississippi. In 1992, he was appointed artistic director of Ballet British Columbia.

Sports

Many Black Canadians have turned to sports because so few other opportunities to do well were open to them. And although they have had some great moments, the sports world was far from perfect.

In 1945, Canada's first professional Black hockey players laced up their skates. They were Herb Carnegie (centre), his brother Ossie (right wing), and Manny McIntyre (left wing), and they played on the same

The Amber Valley Baseball team (Alberta) about 1950.

George Dixon was a boxer from Halifax, Nova Scotia, who became the World's Feather-weight Champion in 1890.

Sylvia Sweeney

offensive line for the Sherbrooke Randies in the Quebec Senior Provincial League.

Herb Carnegie, who was born in 1919 in Toronto, said, "We filled the rinks wherever we went." The three players remained with the Randies until 1947, and then switched over to the Sherbrooke Saints of the Quebec Senior Hockey League. Herb, who later changed teams again to play for the Quebec Aces, said he was always among the top ten goal scorers in his leagues, and that his biggest disappointment was not getting a chance to play in the National Hockey League. "As Black players, we were ignored. We were never invited to try out."

Many excellent Black boxers have come out of Canada. Nova Scotia has been home to most of them. Sam Langford, born in 1884 at Weymouth Falls, Nova Scotia, is still considered one of the best heavyweight boxers ever to step into a ring. He never had the chance to fight for the world championship, but he held the heavyweight championships of England, Spain and Mexico. Langford was only 167 cm tall. In 1906, when he weighed only 71 kg., he took on Jack Johnson, who held the title as the Negro Heavyweight Champion of the world. Johnson, who was 14 kg. heavier, won the fight—but not until the end of 15 hard rounds.

Black women have also excelled in sport. Sylvia Sweeney, who was born in Montreal and lives in Richmond Hill, Ontario, played for the Canadian women's Olympic basketball team in 1976 and 1984. At the time, she was one of the best players in the world. In 1979, Sweeney was voted the most valuable player at the world championships in women's basketball in Seoul, Korea. Sweeney is the niece of Oscar Peterson, the great Canadian pianist. Sweeney is now a film producer, and in 1992 produced "In the Key of Oscar", an acclaimed television special about her uncle.

In 1990, Charmaine Crooks of North Vancouver became the first Canadian woman to run 800 metres in less than 2 minutes. Her time of 1:58.52 set a Canadian record. That year, she was ranked as the fifth-fastest woman in the world in the 800 and the sixth-fastest in the 400 metres. Crooks, who was born in Mandeville, Jamaica, competed for Canada in the 800 metres in the Barcelona Olympics in 1992.

In his day, Harry Jerome was one of the finest 100-metre sprinters in the world. He ran in three Olympic Games and won a bronze medal in the 1964 Tokyo Olympics. He also won the 1967 Pan-American Games. Jerome was born in Prince Albert, Saskatchewan in 1940; and died in Vancouver in 1982.

In 1991, Ferguson Jenkins became the first Canadian inducted into the Baseball Hall of Fame. Jenkins, of Chatham, Ontario had an outstanding career as a pitcher for teams such as the Chicago Cubs, the Texas Rangers and the Boston Red Sox. He won 284 games and struck out 3,192 batters during his career.

Ferguson Jenkins

Jackie Robinson was the first Black American to play modern, major-league baseball. Before he broke into the big leagues, Robinson played in 1946 for the Montreal Royals, which was a farm team of the Brooklyn Dodgers, now the Los Angeles Dodgers. Montrealers treated Robinson like a king and he loved the city for the respect that it had shown him.

Grant Fuhr has been one of the few Blacks to play in the National Hockey League. He was

Grant Fuhr

the first choice of the Edmonton Oilers in the 1981 Entry Draft. He won the Vezina Trophy (1987- 1988); he has played in several Canada Cup Series and All-Star Games; and was a member of five Stanley Cup winners with the Edmonton Oilers.

On November 2, 1991, the West Indies Test Team played the All-Star team from the rest of the world at the Skydome in Toronto. The West Indies Test Team won. About 19,000 spectators watched the game.

Mike Smith, originally of Kenora, Ontario, is one of the world's best decathletes. Smith won a gold medal in the decathlon at the 1990 Commonwealth Games and a silver medal at the 1991 World Championships. In 1991, he also won the Gotzis Decathlon in Austria, which is considered the most important decathlon competition in the world. He participated in the 1992 Olympics in Barcelona, Spain, but was injured and unfortunately had to drop out.

Beyond Today

In their struggles to win freedom and equal treatment, build communities, educate themselves, pursue religious interests and forge ahead in the working world, African-Canadians have known 400 years of trials and triumphs. In their desire to lead lives of peace, dignity and prosperity, Black people continue to face challenges, some of which are unique to their rich yet painful history, and others of which they share with citizens around the world. But there remains room to hope that African-Canadians, and their brothers and sisters of all races and nationalities, will find the courage and the wisdom to make this a better world to live in.

Learning about their new home: an immigrant mother and daughter read the information plaques that outline Manitoba's history at the Forks National Historic Site in Winnipeg.

Important Events in Canadian Black History

In the 400 years that they have lived in Canada, Blacks have been part of many important milestones in Canada's history and culture. The following is a list of highlights.

1604-06 Mattieu da Costa travels with the Champlain expedition to Port Royal. He serves as an interpreter between the French and the Micmac Indians of the area.

1628 Olivier Le Jeune, an 8-year-old boy from Madagascar, arrives in Quebec. He is the first recorded slave purchase in New France. Le Jeune is probably the first person of African origin to live most of his life in Canada.

1709 In New France, slavery becomes legal.

1734 A Montreal slave named Marie-Joseph Angélique learns that she is to be sold to someone else. In an attempt to escape, she sets a fire in her mistress's house. The fire can not be contained, causing damage to half of Montreal. She is caught, tortured and hanged, bringing attention to the conditions of the slaves.

1783 More than 5,000 Blacks leave the United States to live in the Maritimes, Quebec and Ontario. Having sided with the British during the American War of Independence, they come to Canada as United Empire Loyalists, some as free men and some as slaves. Although promised land by the British, they receive only varying amounts of poor-quality land, and, in fact, some receive none at all.

About 1783 In Annapolis Royal, Nova Scotia, Rose Fortune becomes Canada's first policewoman.

1792 A large number of the Black Loyalists in New Brunswick and Nova Scotia migrate to Sierra Leone in West Africa, mainly because the promises of land in Canada were not kept by the British.

1793 Under the leadership of Lieutenant-Governor John Graves Simcoe, Upper Canada passes a law to stop people from bringing slaves into Upper Canada. The law also frees slaves who are 25-years old or more. With this act, Upper Canada becomes the first British territory to bring in legislation against slavery, although it does not abolish slavery entirely.

1796 About 600 Blacks from Jamaica are deported to Nova Scotia. Known as Maroons, they help rebuild the Halifax Citadel. In 1800, most of them leave for Sierra Leone, Africa.

War of 1812 Fighting on the same side as White militia and Mohawk Indians, a group of Black soldiers forces American invaders to retreat in the Battle of Queenston Heights.

Some 2,000 Blacks come from the United States to Nova Scotia and New Brunswick during the War of 1812.

1834   At midnight July 31, slavery comes to an end in all British territories, including British North America. To honour this important event, August 1 is celebrated as Emancipation Day in Windsor, Ontario, and elsewhere.

1837   Black militia units participate in putting down the rebellion in Upper Canada.

Early-mid 1800s   More than 30,000 American Blacks escape slavery in the United States and come to Canada. In the United States, the Fugitive Slave Act is passed in 1850. It provides that even free persons can be made a slave if suspected of being a runaway. As a result, more fugitive slaves and free Black persons come to Canada.

1841- 42   The Dawn Settlement in what is now Dresden, Ontario, is established to provide self-help for Blacks in agricultural communities.

1850s   From her home in St. Catharines, Ontario, Harriet Tubman makes 19 trips into the United States to help slaves escape to Canada.

In Ontario, the Common Schools Act is passed providing for separate schools for Blacks and Roman Catholics. This results in the creation of separate schools for Blacks, leading, in some cases, to Whites refusing to have their children attend schools with Blacks. In Hamilton, Ontario, there are riots as some parents try to prevent Blacks from attending schools with White children.

1853   Mary Ann Shadd becomes the first woman in North America to become editor of a newspaper. Working out of Chatham, Ontario, she publishes, edits and writes in the *Provincial Freeman*, a newspaper serving the Black community in Ontario.

1854   Establishment of the African Baptist Association of Nova Scotia.

1856   Formation of the British Methodist Episcopal Church (BME), an all-Black church.

1858   About 600 Blacks from California move to Victoria, British Columbia. One of them, Mifflin Gibbs, later plays a key role in persuading British Columbia to become part of Canada.

1859   Abraham Shadd is elected to the town council in Raleigh, Ontario, and becomes the first African-Canadian elected to public office.

William Hall, born in Hants County, Nova Scotia, becomes the first Nova Scotian and the first Black to win the Victoria Cross for bravery in war. The Victoria Cross is the highest military honour in the British Commonwealth.

1860   The all-Black Victoria Pioneer Rifle Company is formed to defend British Columbia.

William Hall, V.C.

1861   Dr. Anderson Ruffin Abbott becomes the first Canadian-born Black to graduate from medical school.

1872   Elijah McCoy, born in Colchester, Ontario, invents the first of his many devices to oil engines used on trains and in factories. His inventions are so good that many people refuse to buy imitations of his work. They insist on having "The Real McCoy".

1882   John Ware, a Texas cowboy, moves to Alberta. He introduces longhorn cattle into Canada and pioneers the development of rodeo.

1909   Black farmers from Oklahoma start settling in Alberta, Saskatchewan and Manitoba.

1914-18   Black Canadians join combat units and a construction battalion, The Nova Scotia No. 2 Construction Battalion, is formed as a segregated unit in the First World War. They serve with great loyalty, even though the Government of Canada tries to keep Blacks out of the armed forces, and even though Black soldiers are abused, and sometimes physically attacked, just because of their skin colour.

Anderson Ruffin Abbott was a doctor who was born in Toronto in 1837. He served as a Black surgeon for the Union Army during the American Civil War.

1939-45   In the Second World War, authorities again try to keep Blacks out of the armed forces, but Blacks insist on serving their country. Eventually, they join all services of the war, often serving with distinction.

Blacks served with distinction in the world wars, and in all branches of the armed forces.

1946 Carrie Best, of New Glasgow, Nova Scotia, starts publishing a newspaper called *The Clarion*. Later its name changes to *The Negro Citizen*. It continues publication for 10 years. As a publisher and a writer, Carrie Best shows that Blacks often are not treated fairly in Nova Scotia. She shows how they are not served in restaurants, and kept out of theatres. Best helps to get rid of those practices, making Nova Scotia—and Canada—a better place to live.

1955 The Canadian Pacific Railway finally starts to let some Blacks work as railway conductors. Before that time, many Blacks worked on the railway, primarily as porters, but none were allowed to be conductors.

1950-1960 New laws make it illegal to refuse to let people work, to be served in stores or restaurants or to move into a home because of race.

1960s Large numbers of people from the Caribbean start settling in Canada.

1962 Daniel G. Hill, an American-born Black who moved to Canada in 1950, is made the first director of the Ontario Human Rights Commission, the first government agency in Canada set up to protect citizens from discrimination. Hill later becomes chairman of the Commission. Later still, he serves as the Ombudsman of Ontario. He also writes three books, including *The Freedom Seekers: Blacks in Early Canada*.

For years, until the mid-1950s, the only jobs Blacks could get on the railroad was as sleeping-car porters.

The Canadian immigration policy changes, emphasizing that education and skills of the applicant are to be the main criteria for entry into Canada. This leads to the "Point System" in 1967, which is considered more equitable for Blacks.

1963 Leonard Braithwaite is elected to the Ontario legislature, and is the first Black to serve in a provincial legislature in Canada.

1964 Harry Jerome of Vancouver, British Columbia, wins a bronze medal in the 100-metre dash at the Tokyo Olympics. Earlier, he has run the distance in the world record time of 10.0 seconds. In 1971, he is awarded the Order of Canada "for excellence in all fields of Canadian life."

1972 Rosemary Brown of Vancouver, British Columbia, becomes the first Black woman elected to a provincial legislature in Canada.

1974 Dr. Monestime Saint Firmin is elected mayor of Mattawa, Ontario, making him the country's first Black mayor.

1979 Lincoln Alexander, of Hamilton, Ontario, becomes Canada's first Black cabinet minister. He serves as the Minister of Labour in the federal government. From 1985 to 1991, he serves as the Lieutenant-Governor of Ontario.

Rosemary Brown

1984-88   Daurene Lewis serves as Mayor of Annapolis Royal, Nova Scotia. She is the first Black woman to be elected mayor of a Canadian city.

1990   African National Congress leader Nelson Mandela, who has just been freed from a South African jail, visits Canada. He speaks to huge crowds in Montreal and Toronto.

1991   Jean-Bertrand Aristide, the president of Haiti, who was forced out of his country when the military seized power, visits Canada. He meets with Prime Minister Mulroney and is warmly welcomed by the large Haitian community in Montreal, where he had studied at the University of Montreal in the 1980s.

Julius Alexander Isaac, a native of Grenada, is named Chief Justice of the Federal Court of Canada. He becomes the first Black chief justice in Canada and the first to serve on the Federal Court.

Judge Julius Alexander Isaac

Important Events in Black History in the World

The following are just a few great moments in Black history in the world:

• **More than 6,000 years ago,** people begin to hunt, fish and farm in the Nile River Valley in Africa. Egyptian kingdoms later develop in the same area. Many of the citizens of ancient Egypt are Black.

• **218 B.C.:** Hannibal, the great military leader from North Africa, leads thousands of soldiers and a number of elephants over the Alps (a mountain range in modern-day France) and into Italy, where he attacks and defeats the Roman army in several major battles.

• **From about 713 to 1492:** Moslems from North Africa conquer and control most of Spain. Their headquarters are in Granada, where they build the Alhambra, a spectacular palace on a hill. The Alhambra still stands today, and is one of the most famous places to visit in Spain. The North Africans, who were known as Moors, make great improvements to farming, industry, construction, education, art and science in Spain. The Moors also conquer Portugal, but for a shorter period of time.

• **From about 400 to 1500s:** The West African kingdoms of Ghana, Mali and Songhai are formed.

• **About 1350 to 1592:** People from West Africa, North Africa and the Middle East come to study and to teach at the University of Sankore in Timbuktu (in the country now called Mali). Timbuktu becomes the most important centre of learning in Africa, and its university becomes one of the best in the world.

• **1791:** Blacks fight against slavery in Haiti. Slavery ends in Haiti in 1794. In 1804, Haiti becomes an independent country ruled by Blacks. It is the first Caribbean country to achieve independence.

• **1799:** Alexander Pushkin is born in Moscow. Pushkin, a Black man, becomes Russia's most famous poet. He is still considered to be one of the world's greatest writers.

• **1802:** The birth of Alexander Dumas in France. Dumas writes many famous books, including *The Three Musketeers*.

• **1831:** In Southhampton, Virginia, Nat Turner leads the most famous slave revolt in United States history.

• **1834:** Slavery ends in the British Empire, including Canada.

- **1859**: The painter Henry Tanner is born in Pittsburgh, Pennsylvania. The son of a bishop of the African Methodist Episcopal Church, Tanner devotes many of his paintings to religious subjects. He lives for many years in France, and becomes one of America's greatest artists.

  American John Brown leads an attack on a weapons storage building in Harpers Ferry, West Virginia. The idea is to take the weapons and use them to help destroy slavery in the United States. The attack fails. Most of the attackers, including Brown and a White Canadian named Stewart Taylor, are killed during the raid or hung later.

- **1865**: The Union Army wins the American Civil War, ending slavery in the United States.

- **1869**: Joseph H. Rainey of South Carolina becomes the first Black American elected to the United States House of Representatives.

- **1904**: Charles Drew is born in Washington, D.C. He studies medicine at McGill University in Montreal and becomes a famous doctor and surgeon. He makes important discoveries about how to store human blood so that it can be used later in operations. Sadly, he has a car accident in 1950 and dies after a North Carolina hospital refuses to treat him because he is Black.

- **1908**: Marian Anderson is born in Philadelphia, Pennsylvania. She becomes the world's most famous concert singer. From the 1920s to the 1940s, she sings to great applause throughout North America and Europe.

- **1915**: Billie Holiday is born in Baltimore, Maryland. She becomes one of the most famous blues and jazz singers in American history.

- **1917**: Marcus Garvey of Jamaica begins the Universal Negro Improvement Association. It is the first group that brings together Blacks from all over the world. He encourages Blacks to be proud of themselves, and he becomes the most famous Black leader of his time.

- **1936**: Jesse Owens of the United States becomes the first athlete to win four gold medals at the Olympic Games.

- **1950s-1960s**: Most African countries achieve independence.

- **1950**: Gwendolyn Brooks, an American poet, becomes the first Black woman to win the Pulitzer Prize for literature.

- **1957**: Althea Gibson of the United States becomes the first Black to win the Wimbledon tennis championship in Britain. She wins in the women's singles and doubles category, and she does it again in 1958.

- **1963**: Martin Luther King Jr. leads more than 200,000 people in a march in Washington, D.C., to protest against the terrible treatment of Blacks in the United States. At the march, King delivers the famous "I Have A Dream" speech, in which he hopes that one day all people will treat each other with love and dignity.

- **1964**: Nelson Mandela speaks with power and beauty at his South African trial, where he has been accused of trying to destroy the South African government that treats Blacks as inferior human beings. Mandela is sentenced to life in jail and is sent to prison on Robben Island.

- **1967**: Thurgood Marshall becomes the first Black judge appointed to the United States Supreme Court. As a lawyer in 1954, Marshall won a court case that forced schools to let Black students study with Whites. Before that, many Blacks were not allowed to attend schools where Whites studied.

- **1976**: American writer Alex Haley has his book *Roots* published. *Roots* is the famous novel that traces his Black ancestors back to Kunta Kinte, an African who was stolen as a boy from his village of Juffre, The Gambia, shipped to the United States and sold into slavery. The novel is later made into a major television production.

- **1986**: Alice Walker, born in Eatonton, Georgia, in 1944, wins the Pulitzer Prize and the American Book Award for her novel *The Color Purple*, which is later made into a motion picture.

- **1992**: The South African apartheid system, which treats Blacks as inferior citizens, continues to fall apart.

    The poet Derek Walcott, of St. Lucia, becomes the first Caribbean-born writer to win the Nobel Prize for literature.

- **1993**: On January 20, Maya Angelou, author of "I Know Why The Caged Bird Sings", reads a poem, "On the Pulse of Morning", at the inauguration of United States President Bill Clinton. Angelou becomes the second poet in American history—and the first of African ancestry—to read at a Presidential Inauguration.

The following statistics show, as of 1991, how many Canadians immigrants were born in the Caribbean, Bermuda, Guyana and Africa. Many other Black Canadians were born in Canada and they are not included in these tables. Also, note that not all immigrants from the Caribbean, Bermuda, Guyana or Africa are Black. Besides Blacks, some are White and others Asian.

TABLE 1
NUMBER OF PEOPLE LIVING IN CANADA WHO WERE BORN IN THE CARIBBEAN, BERMUDA, GUYANA AND AFRICA, 1991

Caribbean and Bermuda	232,525	Puerto Rico	195
Anguilla	110	St Christopher & Nevis	1,530
Antigua	1,985	St Lucia	1,780
Aruba	550	St Vincent & The Grenadines	4,540
Bahamas	1,105	Trinidad & Tobago	49,385 [3]
Barbados	14,820	Turks & Caicos Islands	40
Bermuda	1,745	Virgin Islands (British)	35
Cayman Islands	95	Virgin Islands (US)	20
Cuba	1,805	**Guyana**	66,055 [4]
Dominica	1,515	**Africa**	166,175 [5]
Dominican Republic	2,780		
Grenada	4,735		
Guadeloupe	130		
Haiti	39,880 [1]	[1] Living in Quebec: 37,210;
Jamaica	102,440 [2]	[2] Living in Ontario: 86,465;
Martinique	305	[3] Living in Ontario: 37,725;
Montserrat	400	[4] Living in Ontario: 57,665;
Netherlands Antilles	590	[5] Living in Ontario: 78,200.

TABLE 2
NUMBER OF PEOPLE LIVING IN EACH PROVINCE OF CANADA, WHO WERE BORN IN THE CARIBBEAN, BERMUDA, GUYANA AND AFRICA, 1991

	CARIBBEAN & BERMUDA	GUYANA	AFRICA
CANADA	232,525	66,055	166,175
Newfoundland	165	60	315
PEI	30	-	35
Nova Scotia	840	55	880
New Brunswick	255	85	545
Quebec	56,970	3,155	46,285
Ontario	153,830	57,665	78,200
Manitoba	4,325	1,270	2,615
Saskatchewan	790	145	1,615
Alberta	8,480	2,385	15,880
British Columbia	6,690	1,225	19,645
Yukon	60	5	40
Northwest Territories	95	15	110

Further Reading

There are many books and materials published about Blacks in Canada. The following is a list of selected publications that are suggested for further reading.

Books:

Bearden, Jim and Butler, Linda J. Shadd, *The Life and Times of Mary Shadd Cary.* Toronto: NC Press, 1977.

Bertley, Leo, *Canada and Its People of African Descent.* Pierrefonds, 1977.

Carter, Velma and Carter, Levero, *The Black Canadians: Their History and Contributions.* Edmonton: Reidmore Books Inc., 1989.

Clairmont, Donald H. and Magill, Dennis William, *Africville: The Life and Death of a Canadian Black Community.* Toronto: McClelland and Stewart, 1974.

Davidson, Basil and the Editors of Time-Life Books, *African Kingdoms. Amsterdam*: Time-Life Books, 1966 and Reprinted 1984.

Davidson, Basil, *The African Slave Trade.* Boston and Toronto: Little Brown and Company, 1980.

Griffiths, John, *The Caribbean.* East Sussex: Wayland Publishers Limited, 1989.

Hill, Daniel G., *The Freedom-Seekers: Blacks in Early Canada.* Agincourt: Book Society of Canada Limited, 1981.

Kilian, Crawford, *Go Do Some Great Thing: The Black Pioneers of British Columbia.* Vancouver: Douglas & McIntyre, 1978.

Lind, Jane, *The Underground Railroad: Ann Maria Weems.* Toronto: Grolier Limited, 1990.

Pachai, Bridglal, *Beneath the Clouds of the Promised Land: The Survival of Nova Scotia's Blacks.* Halifax: The Black Educators Association of Nova Scotia, 1990.

_____, *Peoples of the Maritimes: Blacks* . Tantallon: Four East Publications, 1987.

Spray, W.A., *The Blacks in New Brunswick.* Fredericton: Brunswick Press, 1972.

Thomson, Colin A., *Blacks in Deep Snow: Black Pioneers in Canada.* Don Mills: J.M. Dent and Sons (Canada) Ltd., 1979.

Walker, James and Thorvaldson, Pat, *Identity: The Black Experience in Canada.* 1979. A print accompaniment for the film "Fields of Endless Days".

Walker, James W. St. G., *A History of Blacks in Canada: A Study Guide for Teachers and Students.* Ottawa: Minister of Supply and Services Canada, 1980.

Winks, Robin, *The Blacks in Canada.* Montreal: McGill-Queens University Press and Yale University Press, 1971.

Index

Picture Credits

The cooperation of persons and organizations in providing photographs, and permission to reproduce them is gratefully appreciated. The page on which each picture appears is listed after each source.
The Honourable Lincoln Alexander, 44; Claus Andersen, 51 top right; Atlantic Records, 48 bottom left; Attic Records, 48 bottom right; Ballet-British Columbia (Cylla von Tiedemann), 49 top right; Black Cultural Centre for Nova Scotia, 32, 33, 56 top; Leonard Braithwaite, 36 top; Rosemary Brown, 56 bottom; The Caribbean Cultural Committee, 38; Chatham-Kent Museum, 22, 51 top left; Rita Cox, 47 top; Forks Renewal Corporation, 52; Cassie Gairdner, 64; Garvey Institute, 36 bottom; Al Gilbert, F.R.P.S. and Regal Recordings Ltd., 47 bottom; Glenbow Archives, 49 bottom; Chief Justice Julius Isaac, 57; Daurene Lewis, 43; Metropolitan Toronto Library Board, 17 (Broadside Collection), 24 top, 24 bottom, 25 top, 34, 42; National Film Board Production "Fields of Endless Day", 21; North American Black Historical Museum, 26, 29 bottom, 45 (Henry Bibb), 45 (The Reverend Samuel Ringgold Ward), 55 top; Ontario Black Historical Society, 13 bottom, 20 bottom, 29 top, 45 (Voice of the Fugitive) Burton Historical Collection, 45 (Provincial Freeman) Daniel Hill Collection, 55 bottom (Wilson Brooks Collection); Ontario Ministry of Tourism, 31; Kenneth H. Pearson, 13 top; Penguin Books Canada Ltd., 49 top left; Propas Management Corporation, 48 top; Public Archives of Canada, 20 top, 27, 28 top (C37966); Public Archives of Nova Scotia, 15 (Newspaper Collection), 30 (Bob Brooks), 46, 50 top, 54; Gwen Robinson, 25 bottom, 35; Saskatchewan Archives Board, 28 bottom (R-A7691); Sylvia Sweeney, 50 bottom; Toronto Maple Leafs, 51 bottom